FAST AND SIMPLE DIABETES RECIPES COOKBOOK

Delicious and Healthy Recipes for Managing Diabetes

Ryan P. Bowser

INTRODUCTION

The illness known as diabetes mellitus is characterized by abnormally high amounts of glucose (blood sugar) in the blood of a person. There are two varieties of diabetes: type 1 diabetes, also known as juvenile diabetes, and type 2 diabetes, which was once known as adult-onset diabetes. Type 1 diabetes refers to diabetes that occurs in children and adolescents. According to a survey, over 28.1 million people and nearly 586,000 children in the United States were diagnosed with diabetes in the year 2015. This represents 2.8% of the total population. A further 86.4 million adults and 8.6 million children, which accounts for approximately 10.6% of the total population of the United States, are estimated to have prediabetes, according to the Centers for Disease Control and Prevention (CDC). There is no correlation between being overweight and developing type 1 diabetes, which typically manifests itself unexpectedly in children, adolescents, and young adults. In cases where a person has a high blood glucose level, it is frequently diagnosed, but this is not always the case. Insulin injections are very necessary for the treatment of this kind of diabetes, which cannot be prevented. It is common for type 2 diabetes to begin gradually and gradually worsen over time. It is an issue that is caused by a lifestyle that is sedentary and bad nutrition. If a person is diagnosed with diabetes, particularly type 2 diabetes, they are given the recommendation to begin following a healthy diet and engaging in a significant amount of physical activity. Additionally, they are instructed to be aware of their target blood glucose levels and to maintain these levels within the blood, and they should undergo frequent blood glucose testing. This will make it possible for them to self-regulate their blood glucose levels effectively, and it will also assist their body in becoming more effective at regulating glucose levels on its own. A diet that is low in fiber is typically consumed by unhealthy eaters, and unhealthy foods are typically high in both fat and carbohydrates. Foods that are high in saturated fats, cholesterol, and trans fats can all contribute to insulin resistance, which in turn raises blood glucose levels. Hyperglycemia can be caused by a variety of illnesses, and it can be used to conceal diabetes. Additionally, various conditions that are connected with hyperglycemia can lead to diabetic ketoacidosis or diabetic coma. Diabetes can lead to severe health issues if it is not treated properly.

These implications might include heart disease, blindness, renal failure, and even the amputation of toes or feet. This book will discuss the most effective methods for managing diabetes.

DIABETES TREATMENT

The treatment options for diabetes are different based on the type of complications, the number of problems, and the severity of the complications, as well as the patient's overall health. Fortunately, diabetes has been the subject of a significant amount of research within the medical world, which has resulted in an abundance of resources and treatments being made available. Insulin supplements are very important for those who have type 1 diabetes. Some people with type 1 diabetes opt to use an insulin pump, which is more expensive but easier to use. Type 1 diabetics rely on regular insulin injections. Because the insulin requirements of type 1 diabetics can change during the day as a result of their eating habits and physical activity, a significant number of type 1 diabetics routinely check their blood sugar levels to determine whether or not their insulin requirements are being met. After years of receiving insulin injections, some people with type 1 diabetes acquire insulin resistance. As a result, oral diabetes medicine, such as metformin, is becoming significantly more routinely recommended to these individuals in order to assist in the prevention of insulin resistance. It is possible to manage type 2 diabetes without the use of medication in certain circumstances. The majority of people who have type 2 diabetes are able to self-regulate their blood sugar levels by eating carefully and engaging in some modest activity. It is suggested that the majority of people who have type 2 diabetes continue to follow diets that are low in fat and high in fiber and healthy carbs. Some people with type 2 diabetes do require medication. insulin is not nearly as typically required for type 2 diabetes as it is for type 1 diabetes; nonetheless, some people with type 2 diabetes do require insulin to complement the lower amount that their pancreas may deliver their body. The medicine metformin is the one that is prescribed to type 2 diabetics the most frequently. By lowering blood glucose levels and improving insulin sensitivity, this medication is available only with a prescription. Sulfonylureas, thiazolidinediones, and meglitinides are some of the other medications that are provided to people who have type 2 diabetes. These medications all promote an increase in insulin production or sensitivity.

Causes of diabetes

Measles, cytomegalovirus, Epstein-Barr virus, and coxsackievirus are examples of viruses that can cause insulin-producing cells in the pancreas to be affected. Although the reasons of some cases are unknown, even very minor viral infections can have this effect. However, the most important risk factors for type 2 diabetes are being overweight or obese, having a family history of the condition (which raises the likelihood of developing type 2 diabetes), being of a certain ethnicity (the highest number of cases is recorded in the populations of sub-Saharan Africa and the Middle East and North Africa), having an incorrect lifestyle (a sedentary lifestyle and obesity), having gestational diabetes (diabetes that occurs during pregnancy), being of a certain age (type 2 diabetes increases with increasing age, particularly after the age of 65), adopting a diet high in fat that encourages obesity, drinking alcohol, and leading a sedentary lifestyle.

Tips to control diabetes

1. **Reduce your intake of salt**: Since it can raise your blood pressure, which raises your risk of heart disease and stroke.
2. **Swap out sugar**: Use sweeteners with no calories in place of sugar. You have far more

control over your blood sugar levels when you cut out sweets.

3. **Eliminate alcohol**: Alcohol has a tendency to be heavy in calories and can produce sharp decreases in blood sugar when consumed on an empty stomach while taking insulin.
4. **Engage in physical activity**: Engaging in physical activity enhances your body's natural glucose burning rate and reduces your chance of cardiovascular problems.
5. **Ten Pointers Steer clear of saturated fats**: These fats, which are found in butter and pastries, can cause excessive cholesterol and problems with blood circulation.
6. **Use olive or canola oil**: If you must use oil for cooking, choose olive or canola oil. Both have a lot of monounsaturated fat and healthy fatty acids. Water is the healthiest beverage by far, so sip it. Water consumption aids in the control of insulin and blood sugar levels. Make sure you consume adequate vitamin D as it is essential for regulating blood sugar levels. Consume foods rich in this vitamin or discuss supplementation with your physician.
7. **Steer clear of processed foods**: These items typically contain high levels of salt,

vegetable oils, refined carbohydrates, and other unhealthy ingredients.

8. **Drink tea and coffee**: These beverages not only help dieters reduce their appetites, but they also include vital antioxidants that support cell protection.

Blood sugar table

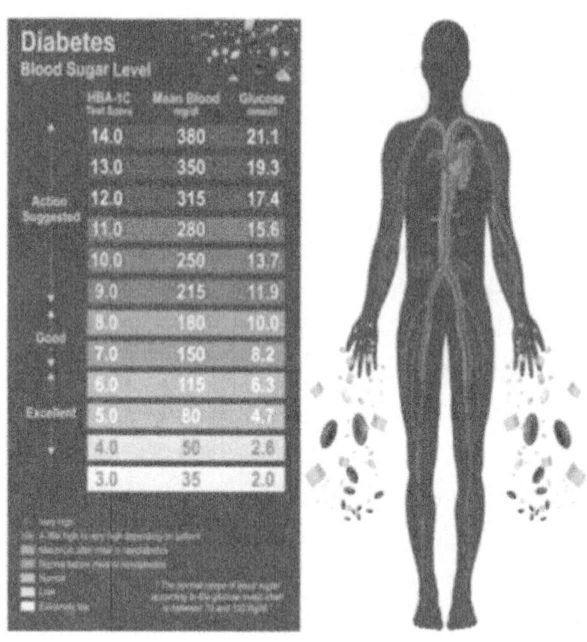

HBA-1C	Mean Blood	Glucose
14.0	380	21.1
13.0	350	19.3
12.0	315	17.4
11.0	280	15.6
10.0	250	13.7
9.0	215	11.9
8.0	180	10.0
7.0	150	8.2
6.0	115	6.3
5.0	80	4.7
4.0	50	2.6
3.0	35	2.0

BREAKFAST

Apple walnut pancakes

Prep Time: 15min
Cook Time: 10min
Serving: 12

Ingredients

1. 1 peeled apple and diced
2. 2 cup of skim milk
3. 2 whites eggs
4. 1 egg, beaten
5. 1 cup of flour
6. 1 cup of whole wheat flour
7. ½ cup of walnuts, chopped
8. 2 tablespoons of sunflower oil
9. 1 tablespoons of Splenda brown sugar
10. 2 teaspoons of baking powder
11. 1 teaspoon of salt
12. Nonstick cooking spray

Directions

1. Add the dry ingredients to a large bowl.
2. Egg whites, egg, milk, and oil should be mixed together in a separate dish before being added to the dry ingredients.
3. The ingredients should be stirred until they are moistened.
4. Apple and walnuts should be folded in. Add some cooking spray, then heat the mixture.

5. On a heated griddle, pour a quarter cup of the batter.
6. When bubbles begin to develop on top, flip the bottle.
7. Prepare until the second side is a golden brown color.
8. Include sugar-free syrup in the serving.

Nutrition

Calories 120
Total Carbs 15 gram
Net Carbs 13 gram
Protein 4 gram
Fat 5 gram
Sugar 3 gram
Fiber 2 gram

Blueberry Cinnamon Muffins

Prep Time: 10min
Cook Time: 30min
Serving: 8

Ingredients

1. 3 eggs
2. 1 cup of blueberries
3. ⅓ cup half-n-half
4. ¼ cup of margarine, melted
5. 1 ½ cup of almond flour

6. ⅓ cup of Splendid
7. 1 teaspoons of baking powder
8. 1 teaspoons of cinnamon

Directions

1. Prepare the oven to a temperature of 350 degrees.
2. Paper liners should be used to line ten muffin cups.

3. Consolidate the following dry ingredients in a large mixing bowl.
4. Add the wet ingredients and thoroughly combine them.
5. Mix in the blueberries, then scoop them out evenly into the muffin tin that has been prepared.
6. The toothpick test must be passed after 25 to 30 minutes in the oven.

Nutritions

Calories 194
Total Carbs 12 gram
Net Carbs 10 gram
Protein 5 gram
Fat 14 gram
Fiber 2 gram
Sugr 9 gram

Berry Breakfast Bark

Prep time: 10min
Cook Time: 2hr
Serving: 6

Ingredients

1. 3-4 strawberries, sliced
2. 1 ½ cup of plain Greek yogurt

3. ½ cup of blueberries
4. ½ cup of low fat granola
5. 3 tablespoons of sugar free maple syrup

Directions

1. Place parchment paper on a baking pan and set it aside.
2. To combine the yogurt and syrup, mix them together in a basin of medium size.

3. Spread the mixture out in a thin layer in the pan that has been prepared.
4. Put the remains on top.
5. Parts and pieces.
6. Wrap in aluminum foil and place in the freezer for two hours or overnight.
7. In order to serve, cut the cake into squares and serve it right away.
8. It is possible for bark to lose its shape if it thaws too much.
9. Any remaining bark should be placed in a container that is airtight and placed in the freezer.

Nutritions

Calories 69
Total Carbs 18 gram
Net Carbs 16 gram
Protein 7 gram
Fat 6 gram
Sugar 7 gram
Fiber 2 gram

Breakfast Pizza

Prep Time: 10min
Cook Time: 25min
Serving: 6

Ingredients

1. 12 eggs
2. ½ lb breakfast sausage
3. 1 cup of bell pepper, sliced
4. 1 cup of red pepper, sliced
5. 1 cup of cheddar cheese, grated
6. ½ cup of half-n-half
7. ½ teaspoons of salt
8. ¼ teaspoons of pepper

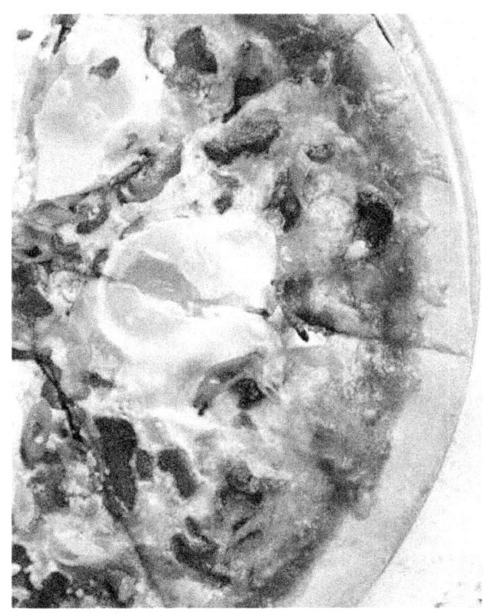

Directions

1. Prepare the oven to a temperature of 350 degrees.
2. Sausage should be browned in a skillet. Move the contents to the basin.

3. Cook the peppers for three to five minutes, or until they start to become more pliable.
4. Move the mixture to a bowl.
5. The eggs, cream, salt, and pepper should be mixed together in a small bowl using a whisk. Transfer to the skillet.
6. Wait five minutes, or until the sides begin to set, before serving.
7. 30 minutes in the oven. Remove it from the oven and place it in the broiler.
8. The "crust" should be topped with cheese, peppers, and sausage.
9. Under the broiler, cook the cheese until it begins to melt and turns brown.
10. Before slicing and serving, allow the meat to rest.

Nutritions

Calories 230

Total Carbs 4 gram

Protein 16 gram

Fat 17 gram

Sugar 2 gram

Fiber 0 gram

Cauliflower Breakfast Hash

Prep Time: 10min
Cook Time: 18min
Serving: 2

Ingredients

1. 4 cups of cauliflower, grated
2. 1 cup of mushrooms, diced
3. ¾ cup of onion, diced
4. 3 slices bacon
5. ¼ cup of sharp cheddar cheese, grated

Directions

1. After frying the bacon in a skillet of medium size over medium-high heat, leave it aside.

2. Place the vegetables in the skillet and heat them until they reach a golden brown color, turning them regularly.
3. To reintroduce the bacon to the skillet, cut it into pieces.
4. Put some cheese on top, and then wait for it to melt.
5. Serve as soon as possible.

Nutritions

Calories 155
Total Carbs 16 gram
Net Carbs 10 gram
Protein 10 gram
Fat 7 gram
Sugar 7 gram
Fiber 6 gram

Cafe Mocha Smoothies

Prep Time: 10min
Cook Time: 5min
Serving: 3

Ingredients

1. 1 ½ avocado, remove pit and cut in half
2. 1 ½ cup of almond milk, unsweetened
3. ½ cup of canned coconut milk

4. 3 tablespoons of Splendid
5. 3 tablespoons of unsweetened cocoa powder
6. 2 teaspoons of instant coffee
7. 1 teaspoons of vanilla

Directions

1. Put everything in the blender, with the exception of the avocado.
2. Maintain a smooth consistency.

3. Add the avocado and blend until it is completely smooth and there are no bits left.
4. To serve, pour the mixture into glasses.

Nutritions

Calories 109
Total Carbs 15 gram
Protein 6 gram
Fat 1 gram
Sugar 13 gram
Fiber 0 gram

Cinnamon Apple Granola

Prep Time: 5min
Cook Time: 35min
Serving: 4

Ingredients

1. 1 apple, peel and dice fine
2. ¼ cup of margarine, melted
3. 1 cup of walnuts or pecans
4. 1 cup of almond flour
5. ⅗ cup of flaked coconut
6. ½ cup of sunflower seeds
7. ½ cup of hemp seeds
8. ⅓ cup of Splendid
9. 2 teaspoons of cinnamon

10. 2 teaspoons of vanilla
11. ½ teaspoons of salt

Directions

1. Bring the temperature of the oven up to 300 degrees.
2. Place parchment paper on a large baking sheet and set it aside.
3. It is recommended that you use a food processor to combine the nuts, flour, coconut, seeds, Splendid, and salt.

4. Process the ingredients until it resembles coarse crumbs, but it should still contain some lumps. Transfer to a bowl, then add cinnamon and apple to the mixture.
5. Add the vanilla extract and margarine and stir until the mixture is well coated and begins to clump together.
6. Spread the mixture out evenly on the pan that has been prepared.
7. Stir it a couple of times while it is baking for twenty-five minutes, or until it begins to brown.
8. After turning off the oven, let the granola remain inside for five to ten minutes.
9. After removing it from the oven, let it cool fully,as it cools, it will become more crisp. Place in a container that is airtight.

Nutritions

Calories 360
Total Carbs 19 gram
Net Carbs 14 gram
Protein 10 gram
Fat 28 gram
Sugar 12 gram
Fiber 5 gram

Cinnamon Rolls

Prep Time: 15min
Cook Time: 20min
Serving: 6

Ingredients

1. 4 eggs
2. 1 ripe banana
3. ⅔ cup of coconut flour
4. 6 tablespoons of honey, divided
5. 6 tablespoons of coconut oil, soft, divided
6. 1 teaspoons of vanilla
7. 1 teaspoons of baking soda
8. ½ teaspoons of salt
9. 1 tablespoon and ½ teaspoons of cinnamon

Directions

1. Prepare the oven to a temperature of 350 degrees.
2. Place parchment paper on a cookie sheet and set it aside.
3. The eggs should be lightly beaten in a medium basin.
4. Bananas should be beaten in. Mix in two tablespoons of honey, two tablespoons of melted coconut oil, and vanilla extract until everything is incorporated.
5. After carefully combining the flour, salt, baking soda, and half a teaspoon of cinnamon, mix in the remaining ingredients.
6. If you find that the dough is too sticky, gradually add more flour to the mixture.
7. After preparing a work surface with parchment paper, place the dough on top of the surface.
8. A mixture of two tablespoons of honey, two tablespoons of coconut oil, and one tablespoon of cinnamon should be mixed together in a small bowl and then put on dough.
9. Create a roll and then cut it into six equal pieces. Place in the prepared pan and bake

for fifteen to thirty minutes, or until the top is golden brown.

10. You should wait ten minutes.
11. The remaining two teaspoons of honey and coconut oil should be mixed together, and then spread over the rolls that are still warm.
12. Then served

Nutritions

Calories 247
Total Carbs 23 gram
Protein 4 gram
Fat 17 gram
Sugar 20 gram
Fiber 1 gram

LUNCH

Cilantro Lime Shrimp

Prep Time: 15min
Cook Time: 8min
Serving: 4

Ingredients

1. ½ teaspoon of garlic clove, minced
2. 1 pound (454 g) large shrimp, peeled and deveined
3. ¼cup of chopped fresh cilantro
4. 1 lime, zested and juiced
5. 1 teaspoon extra of virgin olive oil
6. ¼ teaspoon of salt
7. ⅛ teaspoon of black pepper

Directions

1. To reheat the olive oil, place it in a big skillet that is heavy and heat it over medium-high heat.
2. After thirty seconds, add the garlic that has been minced and continue to heat until the aroma is released.

3. Add the shrimp and cook them for around five to six minutes, stirring them occasionally, or until they become pink and opaque according to your preference.
4. In a bowl, remove the mixture from the heat.
5. To the shrimp, add the cilantro, lime zest and juice, salt, and pepper, and toss this mixture until it is well distributed.
6. Serve as soon as possible.

Nutritions

Calories 133
Fat 3.5 gram
Protein 24.3 gram
Carbs 1.0 gram
Fiber 0 gram
Sugar 0 gram
Sodium 258 milligram

Lemon Parsley White Fish Fillets

Prep time: 10min
Cook Time: 10min
Serving: 4

Ingredients

1. 4 (170-g) lean of white fish filets, rinsed and patted dry

2. 2 tablespoons of parsley, finely chopped
3. ½ teaspoon of lemon zest
4. ¼ of teaspoon dried dill
5. 1 medium lemon, halved
6. Cooking spray
7. Paprika, to taste
8. Salt and pepper, to taste
9. ¼ cup of extra virgin olive oil

Directions

1. Preheat the oven to 400 degrees Fahrenheit (205 degrees Celsius).
2. Apply cooking spray to a baking sheet that has been covered with aluminum foil and set aside.
3. Paprika should be sprinkled over the filets after they have been placed on the foil.
4. Use salt and pepper to season the food to your liking.

5. In an oven that has been warmed, bake the meat for ten minutes, or until it can be easily flaked apart with a fork.
6. While this is going on, in a separate bowl, combine the dill, olive oil, lemon zest, and parsley by stirring them together.
7. After taking the fish out of the oven, place it on four plates.
8. Squeeze the lemon juice over the fish, and then spoon the parsley mixture on top of the fish before serving.

Nutritions

Calories 283
Fat 17.2 gram
Protein 33.3 gram
Carbs 1.0 gram
Fiber 0 gram
Sugar 0 gram
Sodium 74 milligram

Asparagus and Scallop Skillet with Lemony

Prep Time: 10min
Cook Time: 15min
Serving: 4

Ingredients

1 pound (454 g) asparagus, trimmed and cut into 2-inch segments 1 pound (454 g) sea scallops
1/4 cup dry white wine
2 garlic cloves, minced
Juice of 1 lemon
From the Cupboard:
3 teaspoons extra-virgin olive oil, divided 1 tablespoon butter
1/4 teaspoon freshly ground black pepper

Directions

1. One-half of the olive oil should be heated in a skillet that does not stick over medium heat until it shimmers.
2. To the skillet, add the asparagus, and sauté it for six minutes, or until it becomes tender.
3. After the asparagus has been cooked, place it on a big platter and cover it with aluminum foil.
4. Melt the butter in the skillet by heating the other half of the olive oil and butter until the butter is completely melted.
5. The scallops should be cooked for six minutes, or until they become opaque and browned, after being attached to the skillet.
6. The scallops should be turned over with tongs at the halfway point of the cooking time.
7. Once the scallops have been transferred to the platter, cover them with aluminum foil on top.
8. The wine, garlic, lemon juice, and black pepper should all be mixed together in the skillet.
9. Simmer for two minutes on a heat setting of medium-low. Stir the mixture frequently while it is cooking.

10. After thoroughly coating the asparagus and scallops with the sauce, serve them while they are still warm.

Nutritions

Calories 256
Fat 6.9 gram
Protein 26.1 gram
Carbs 14.9 gram
Fiber 2.1 gram
Sugar 2.9 gram
Sodium 491 milligram

Creamy Cod Fillet with Quinoa and Asparagus

Prep Time: 5min
Cook Time: 15min
Serving: 4

Ingredients

1. ½ cup of uncooked quinoa
2. 4 (113-g) cod of filets
3. ½ teaspoon of garlic powder, divided
4. 24 asparagus spears, cut the bottom 1 ½ inches off
5. 1 cup half-and-half
6. ¼ teaspoon of salt

7. ¼ teaspoon of freshly ground black pepper
8. 1 tablespoon of avocado oil

Directions

1. Place the quinoa in a pot of water that has been seasoned.
2. Assume a boiling point.
3. For fifteen minutes, or until the quinoa is tender and has a white "tail," reduce the heat to a low setting and simmer the mixture.
4. Switch off the heat and cover the pot. Have it sit for five minutes.
5. The cod filets should be rubbed with a quarter teaspoon of garlic powder, salt, and pepper on a surface that has been thoroughly cleaned.
6. The avocado oil should be heated in a skillet that does not stick over medium-low heat.

7. In a skillet, add the cod filets and asparagus, and cook them for eight minutes, or until they reach the desired level of tenderness.
8. During the middle of the cooking period, turn the fish over and shake the skillet occasionally.
9. After pouring the half-and-half into the skillet, sprinkle the remaining garlic powder on top of the mixture.
10. Turn the heat up to high and let it simmer for two minutes, or until it reaches a creamy consistency.
11. Asparagus, cod filets, and quinoa should be divided among four bowls and served at a warm temperature.

Nutritions

Calories 258
Fat 7.9 gram
Protein 25.2 gram
Carbs 22.7 gram
Fiber 5.2 gram
Sugar 3.8 gram
Sodium 410 milligram

Wilted Dandelion Greens with Sweet Onion

Prep Time: 15min
Cook Time: 12min
Serving: 4

Ingredients

1. 1 Vidalia of onion, thinly sliced
2. 2 garlic of cloves, minced
3. 2 bunches of dandelion greens, roughly chopped
4. ½ cup of low-sodium vegetable broth
5. 1 tablespoon extra-virgin olive oil
6. Freshly ground black pepper, to taste

Directions

1. Be sure to warm the olive oil.

2. The onion and garlic should be cooked for two to three minutes, tossing them occasionally, until they are soft.
3. When the dandelion greens have reached the desired level of wilting, add the broth and continue to boil for five to seven minutes while tossing the mixture often.
4. Place on a platter, and then douse with freshly ground black pepper. Serve when still heated.

Nutritions

Calories 81
Fat 3.8 gram
Protein 3.1 gram
Carbs 10.7 gram
Fiber 3.8 gram
Sugar 2.0 gram
Sodium 72 milligram

Asparagus with Scallops

Prep Time: 10min
Cook Time: 15min
Serving: 4

Ingredients

1. 1 pound (454 g) asparagus, trimmed and cut into 2-inch segments
2. 1 pound (454 g) sea scallops
3. ½ cup dry of white wine
4. Juice of 1 lemon
5. 2 garlic cloves, minced
6. 3 teaspoons extra-virgin olive oil, divided
7. 1 tablespoon butter
8. ¼ teaspoon freshly ground black pepper

Directions

1. One and a half tablespoons of oil should be heated within a large skillet over medium heat.

2. Once the asparagus has been added, sauté it for five to six minutes, turning it frequently, until it is just soft.
3. To maintain the temperature, remove the food from the skillet and cover it with aluminum foil.
4. After adding the butter and the remaining 1 1/2 teaspoons of oil, the skillet should be ready to use.
5. The scallops should be arranged in a single layer in the skillet once the butter has melted and is sizzling.
6. Prepare on one side till it has a lovely brown color.
7. Using tongs, carefully loosen and flip the scallops, and then continue cooking them for another three minutes on the other side, until they are browned and cooked all the way through.
8. Remove the foil and cover it with it to keep it warm. The wine, lemon juice, garlic, and pepper should all be mixed together in the same skillet.
9. For one to two minutes, bring to a simmer while stirring to include any browned parts that may still be present in the pan.

10. Place the scallops and asparagus that have been cooked back into the skillet so that they may be coated with the sauce.
11. Serve when still heated.

Directions

Calories 253
Fat 7.1 gram
Protein 26.1 gram
Carbs 14.9 gram
Fiber 2.1 gram
Sugar 3.1 gram
Sodium 494 milligram

Butter Cod with Asparagus

Prep Time: 5min
Cook Time: 10min
Serving: 4

Ingredients

1. 4 (113-g) cod filets
2. ¼ teaspoon of garlic powder
3. 24 asparagus spears, woody ends trimmed
4. ½ cup of brown rice, cooked
5. 1 tablespoon freshly squeezed lemon juice
6. ¼ teaspoon salt

7. ¼ teaspoon freshly ground black pepper
8. 2 tablespoons unsalted butter

Directions

1. Salt, pepper, and garlic powder should be used to season the cod filets, which should be placed in a big bowl.
2. Put aside for later.
3. In a skillet, melt the butter by heating it over medium-low settings.

4. While the cod filets and asparagus are cooking, arrange them in a single layer in the skillet.
5. Cook the cod with the lid on for eight minutes, or until it is completely cooked through.
6. Place the brown rice that has been cooked, the fish filets, and the asparagus on each of the four plates.
7. Serve with the lemon juice sprinkled over the top.

Nutritions

Calories 233
Fat 8.2 gram
Protein 22.1 gram
Carbs 20.1 gram
Fiber 5.2 gram
Sugar 2.2 gram
Sodium 275 milligram

DINNER

Broccoli and Hot Sauce

Prep Time: 5min
Cook Time: 5min
Serving: 4

Ingredients

4 cups of broccoli florets
1 tablespoon of extra-virgin olive oil
½ teaspoon of hot sauce
Sea salt to taste
Black ground pepper as needed

Directions

1. Prepare a steamer basket and arrange your broccoli in it.
2. To ensure that your broccoli is tender, steam it for around five minutes.
3. A drizzle of oil, along with a sprinkling of spicy sauce, sea salt, and black pepper, should be put on top.
4. Serve and take pleasure in it!

Nutritions

Calories 30
Protein 4 gram
Fat 0 gram
Carbs 5 gram

Country Breakage Chicken Tenders

Prep Time: 10min
Cook Time: 15min
Serving: 4

Ingredients

1. ¾ lb. of chicken tenders For breading
2. 2 tablespoons of olive oil
3. 1 teaspoon of black pepper
4. ½ teaspoon of salt
5. ½ cup of seasoned breadcrumbs
6. ½ cup of all-purpose flour
7. 2 eggs, beaten

Directions

1. Set your Air Fryer to 330 degrees Fahrenheit.
2. Separate the breadcrumbs, eggs, and flour into three separate bowls and put them aside.
3. Add salt and pepper to the breadcrumbs to give them its flavor.

4. The breadcrumbs should be combined with olive oil and thoroughly mixed.
5. To prepare chicken tenders, first coat them in flour, then dip them in eggs, and then coat them in breadcrumbs.
6. In order to guarantee that the breadcrumbs are distributed uniformly around the chicken, press.
7. The cooking basket should be shaken to remove any excess breading.
8. The chicken tenders should be cooked in the air fryer for a period of ten minutes. Serve when still heated.

Nutritions

Calories 276
Total Fat 8.6 gram
Carbs 7 gram
Protein 13.2 gram

Avocados with Walnut-Herb

Prep Time: 7min
Cook Time: 5min
Serving: 2

Ingredients

1. 1 avocado

2. ¼ cup of walnuts
3. 1 ½ teaspoons of virgin olive oil
4. 1 ½ teaspoons of lemon juice (fresh)
5. 1 tablespoon of fresh basil
6. Sea salt to taste
7. Black pepper to taste

Directions

1. A pan should be used to fry the chopped nuts for around five minutes over medium-low heat.
2. Chilled basil, lemon juice, olive oil, and a pinch each of salt and pepper should be combined in a small bowl.
3. After slicing the avocado in half, sprinkle the walnut mixture on top of the slices, and then serve and enjoy!

Nutritions

Calories 200
Protein 2 gram
Fat 17 gram
Carbs 7 gram

Barbecue Brisket

Prep Time: 15min
Cook Time: 5min
Serving: 4

Ingredients

1 cup of beef broth
2 lb. of beef brisket
1 sweet onion, diced
½ cup of barbecue sauce
½ tablespoon of steak seasoning

Directions

1. Add the prepared onion to your slow cooker. Rub the trimmed brisket with seasoning.
2. Cut the brisket into pieces, and add to your slow cooker.
3. Pour the beef broth and barbecue sauce over the brisket.
4. Cook on low for 5 hours, slice brisket. Serve and enjoy!

Nutritions

Calories 188
Protein 13 gram
Fat 8 gram
Carbs 15 gram

Orange-Avocado Salad

Prep Time: 10min
Cook Time: None
Serving: 2

Ingredients

1. ½ teaspoon of arugula
2. 1 avocado
3. 1 navel orange
4. 1 tablespoon of fresh lime juice
5. 1 tablespoon of extra-virgin olive oil

Directions

1. Mix the lime juice, arugula and oil in a bowl.

2. Add the peeled orange, and then toss.
3. Add the diced avocado just before serving, then enjoy!

Nutritions

Calories 30
Protein 2 gram
Fat 2 gram
Carbs 1 gram

Salmon and Citrus Sauce

Prep Time: 10min
Cook Time: 15min
Serving: 2

Ingredients

¾ lb. of salmon filets
⅓ cup of fresh orange juice
1 tablespoon of fresh lime juice
1 tablespoon of fresh lemon juice
1 tablespoon of honey
1 tablespoon of olive oil
1 ½ tablespoons of mustard
Sea salt along
Black pepper as needed
¼ teaspoon of smoked paprika

Directions

1. Paprika, salt, and pepper should be sprinkled on individual filets.
2. The next step is to cook.
3. The lemon, orange, and lime juices, together with the honey, should be combined and then added to a small pot while the filets are cooking.
4. After adding the mustard and stirring it to mix, continue cooking for ten minutes over a low heat.
5. The salmon filets should be placed in serving dishes, and then the sauce should be poured over the filets.
6. Serve and take pleasure in it!

Nutritions

Calories 210
Protein 20 gram
Fat 22 gram
Carbs 0.3 gram

Beef Tenderloin and Avocado Cream

Prep Time: 9min
Cook Time: 8min
Serving: 2

Ingredients

1. 1 teaspoon of mustard
2. 2 (6 ounces) of beef steaks
3. ¼ cup of sour cream
4. 2 teaspoons of lemon juice, fresh
5. ⅓ of avocado
6. 1 tablespoon of olive oil-slicked
7. Sea salt to taste
8. Ground black pepper as needed

Directions

1. Bring the temperature of your oven up to 450 degrees Fahrenheit.
2. Salt and pepper should be sprinkled on the beef steaks before cooking.

3. Mustard and oil should be combined, and then the mixture should be smeared over the meat.
4. Start by placing the steaks in a skillet and cooking them for three minutes over medium-high heat.
5. After placing the steaks on a baking sheet, place the sheet in the oven, and bake the steaks for a total of six minutes.
6. The avocado, lemon juice, and sour cream should be blended together.
7. Served with avocado cream, steaks are sure to be enjoyed!

Nutritions

Calories 205
Protein 20 gram
Fat 15 gram
Carbs 1 gram

Lemon Cauliflower and Pine Nuts

Prep Time: 5min
Cook Time: 20min
Serving: 4

Ingredients

1. 1 teaspoon of lemon zest

2. ¼ teaspoon of sea salt
3. 1 package of cauliflower florets
4. 2 tablespoons of extra virgin olive oil
5. 2 tablespoons of pine nuts
6. 1 tablespoon of parsley, fresh flat-leaf
7. 1 ½ teaspoons of lemon juice
8. ¼ teaspoon of fresh ground black pepper

Directions

1. Prepare your oven by preheating it to 400 degrees Fahrenheit.
2. Put all of the ingredients into a big bowl and mix them together.
3. Next, place the mixture on a baking pan. 20 minutes into the baking process, serve, and savor!

Nutritions

Calories 60
Protein 4 gram
Fat 0 gram
Carbs 8 gram

Italian Seafood Stew

Prep Time: 20min
Cook Time: 40min
Serving: 4

Ingredients

1. 1 cup of onion, diced
2. 2 garlic of cloves, minced
3. 1 lb. of medium-sized raw shrimp (unpeeled)
4. 1 lb. of cod
5. 1 ½ tablespoons of olive oil
6. 1 cup of water
7. 1 (15 ounces) can tomatoes
8. ½ (1 ounce) of package thyme
9. ½ cup of chicken broth

Directions

1. Garlic and onion that have been minced should be cooked in hot oil for ten minutes in a skillet that is set over medium-high heat.

2. Cook the mixture until the liquid has almost completely evaporated, stirring in the broth and one thyme sprig.
3. Then, after adding the water and crushed tomatoes, let the mixture simmer for twenty minutes.
4. Along with the fish, add shrimp that has been peeled and deveined, and continue to boil for an additional eight minutes.
5. Get rid of the thyme sprigs.
6. Two teaspoons of thyme should be chopped and added to the stew.
7. Serve and take pleasure in it!

Nutritions

Calories 70
Protein 12 gram
Fat 3 gram
Carbs 0 gram

Vegetable Egg Bake

Prep Time: 20min
Cook Time: 30min
Serving: 2

Ingredients

1. 6 large eggs
2. ½ (16 ounces) package Kielbasa
3. ½ cup of red bell pepper, chopped
4. ½ cup of green bell pepper, chopped
5. 1 ½ teaspoons of olive oil
6. ½ (8 ounces) of package mushrooms
7. ⅛ teaspoon of sea salt
8. ¼ teaspoon of fresh ground black pepper

Directions

1. Prepare your oven by preheating it to 400 degrees Fahrenheit.
2. Cook your Kielbasa that has been sliced into pieces measuring half an inch, along with mushrooms and bell peppers that have been

diced, for a period of five minutes over warm to high heat.

3. Take the food out of the skillet. Your eggs, along with the salt and pepper, should be whisked together in a mixing dish.
4. Eggs should be mixed in with the kielbasa mixture, and then the mixture should be poured onto a skillet that is oven-safe and has been lightly buttered.
5. 20 minutes into the baking process, serve, and savor!

Nutritions

Calories 300
Protein 16 gram
Fat 29 gram
Carbs 2 gram

Roasted Vegetable Medley

Prep Time: 10min
Cook Time: 20min
Serving: 4

Ingredients

1. 1 tablespoon of extra-virgin olive oil

2. ½ (8 ounces) package of whole button mushrooms
3. 1 (12 ounces) package of cauliflower, carrot and broccoli mix
4. ¼ teaspoon sea salt

Directions

1. Bring the temperature of your oven up to 450 degrees Fahrenheit.
2. Your vegetables should be tossed in a basin with oil, and then you should season them with salt and pepper to taste.
3. Place a variety of vegetables on a baking pan, and bake them for twenty minutes.
4. Take care and have fun!

Nutritions

Calories 70
Protein 10 gram
Fat 4 gram
Carbs 1 gram

Chicken Salad

Prep Time: 15min
Cook Time: 10min
Serving: 2

Ingredients

1. ½ (10 ounces) package leafy lettuce
2. 1 ½ cups of rotisserie chicken
3. ⅓ cup of almonds, sliced
4. 1 garlic of clove, minced
5. 1 carrot, shredded
6. ½ cucumber, shredded
7. 2 tablespoons of olive oil
8. 1 teaspoon of honey
9. 1 ½ teaspoons of ginger, shredded
10. 1 tablespoon of soy sauce
11. 1 tablespoon of rice vinegar
12. 1 teaspoon of honey

Directions

1. Fry the nuts, and then allow them to cool.
2. Put the chicken, carrots, lettuce, and shredded cucumber into a mixing dish and mix them together.
3. The ginger that has been granted, honey, garlic that has been minced, vinegar, and soy sauce should all be added to a small mixing bowl and mixed together.
4. Once the salad is ready, pour the soy sauce mixture over it, and then serve and enjoy!

Nutritions

Calories 90
Protein 12 gram
Fat 7 gram

Carbs 0 gram

Strawberry-Arugula Salad

Prep Time: 10min
Cook Time: None
Serving: 2

Ingredients

1. ¼ cup of parsley leaves, fresh, chopped
2. 2 cups arugula
3. ½ cup of strawberries
4. ¼ cup of basil leaves, fresh
5. 3 tablespoons of lemon vinaigrette
6. ¼ cup of red onion, thinly sliced
7. thinly sliced almonds (optional) for topping

Directions

1. A salad bowl should be used to combine the parsley, arugula, and basil.
2. Toss the salad once more after adding the dressing, the berries that have been quartered, and the red onion.
3. After the salad has been prepared, season it with salt and pepper to taste, and then sprinkle it with almonds that have been cut very thinly.
4. Serve and take pleasure in it!

Nutritions

Calories 41

Protein 0.2 gram

Fat 0.4 gram

Carbs 20 gram

APPETIZERS

Skillet Turkey Patties

Prep Time: 7min
Cook Time: 8min
Serving: 2

Ingredients

1. ½ lb. of lean ground turkey
2. ½ cup of low-sodium chicken broth
3. ¼ cup of red onion
4. ½ teaspoons of Worcestershire sauce
5. 1 teaspoons of extra virgin olive oil
6. ¼ teaspoons of oregano (dried)
7. ⅛ teaspoons of pepper

Directions

1. The turkey, chopped onion, Worcestershire sauce, dried oregano, and pepper should be combined and then used to make two patties.
2. To prepare the patties, heat the oil and cook them for four minutes on each side.
3. Take the broth and bring it to a boil in the skillet.
4. After two minutes of boiling, ladle sauce over the patties.

Nutritions

Calories 180
Fat 11 gram
Carbohydrates 9 gram

Mushroom Pasta

Prep Time: 7min
Cook Time: 10min
Serving: 4

Ingredients

1. 4 oz of whole-grain linguine
2. 1 teaspoons of extra virgin olive oil

3. ½ cup of light sauce
4. 2 tablespoons of green onion
5. 1 (8-oz) package of mushrooms
6. 1 clove garlic
7. ⅛ teaspoons of salt
8. ⅛ teaspoons of pepper

Directions

1. Follow the instructions on the package to cook the pasta, then drain it.
2. For four minutes, fry the sliced mushrooms. Mix in the minced garlic, salt, and pepper, then stir in the fettuccine.
3. Cook for two minutes.
4. The light sauce should be heated until it is warm; then, the pasta mixture should be topped with the sauce and with lightly chopped green onion.

Nutritions

Calories 300
Fat 1 gram
Carbohydrates 15 gram

Turkey Loaf

Prep Time: 10min
Cook Time: 40min
Serving: 4

Ingredients

1. ½ lb. 93% of lean ground turkey
2. ⅓ cup of panko breadcrumbs
3. ½ cup of green onion
4. 1 egg
5. ½ cup of green bell pepper

6. 1 tablespoons of ketchup
7. ¼ cup of sauce (Picante)
8. ½ teaspoons of cumin (ground)

Directions

1. Bake at 350 degrees Fahrenheit.
2. In a bowl, combine the following ingredients: lean ground turkey, three tablespoons of Picante sauce, panko breadcrumbs, an egg,

chopped green onion, chopped green bell pepper, and cumin; stir thoroughly.

3. After placing the mixture on a baking sheet, form it into an oval with a thickness of around 1.5 inches.
4. Bake for forty-five minutes.
5. Apply the remaining ketchup and Picante sauce to the loaf after mixing them together.
6. Continue baking for a further five minutes.
7. Let it sit for five minutes.

Nutritions

Calories 150
Protein 20 gram
Fat 8 gram

Tomato and Roasted Cod

Prep Time: 10min
Cook Time: 30min
Serving: 2

Ingredients

1. 2 (4-oz) cod of filets
2. 1 cup of cherry tomatoes
3. ⅔ cup of onion
4. 2 teaspoons of orange rind

5. 1 tablespoons of extra virgin olive oil
6. 1 teaspoons of thyme (dried)
7. ¼ teaspoons of salt, divided
8. ¼ teaspoons of pepper, divided

Description

1. Bake at 400 degrees Fahrenheit.

2. To the mixture, add half tomatoes, sliced onion, grated orange rind, extra virgin olive oil, dried thyme, and one eighth of a teaspoon each of salt and pepper.
3. Fry for five minutes.
4. Remove from the oven. Place fish in a single layer on the pan, and season it with the remaining ⅛ teaspoon of salt and pepper.
5. Apply the tomato mixture that was reserved to the fish.
6. For ten minutes, bake.

Nutritions

Calories 120

Protein 9 gram

Fat 2 gram

Chicken Tikka Masala

Prep Time: 5min

Cook Time: 15min

Serving: 2

Ingredients

1. ½ lb. of chicken breasts
2. ¼ cup of onion
3. ⅕ teaspoons of extra virgin olive oil
4. 1 (14.5-oz) can of tomatoes

5. 1 teaspoons of ginger
6. 1 teaspoons of fresh lemon juice
7. ⅓ cup of plain Greek yogurt (fat-free)
8. 1 tablespoons of garam masala
9. ¼ teaspoons of salt
10. ¼ teaspoons of pepper

Directions

1. Add one-half teaspoon of garam masala, one-eighth teaspoon of salt, and one-eighth teaspoon of pepper to chicken that has been cut into cubes of one inch in size.
2. 4 to 5 minutes of cooking time for chicken and diced onion.
3. Put in some chopped tomatoes, some grated ginger, some garam masala, and a little bit of salt.
4. Bake for eight to ten minutes. Blend the yogurt and lemon juice together until smooth.

Nutritions

Calories 200
Protein 26 gram
Fat 10 gram

French Broccoli Salad

Prep Time: 10min
Cook Time: 10min
Serving: 8

Ingredients

1. 8 cups of broccoli florets
2. 3 strips of bacon, cooked and crumbled
3. ¼ cup of sunflower kernels

4. 1 bunch of green onion, sliced
5. 3 tablespoons of seasoned rice vinegar
6. 3 tablespoons of canola oil
7. ½ cup of dried cranberries

Directions

1. Gather the broccoli, cranberries, and green onion into a bowl and mix them together.
2. Using a whisk, combine the oil and vinegar in a separate basin. Mix thoroughly. The broccoli mixture should now be drizzled over.
3. Coat thoroughly by throwing it.
4. The bacon and sunflower kernels should be sprinkled on top before serving.

Nutritions

Calories 121
Carbohydrates 14 gram
Cholesterol 2 milligram

Fiber 3 gram
Sugar 1 gram
Fat 7 gram
Protein 3 gram
Sodium 233 milligram

Tenderloin Grilled Salad

Prep Time: 10min
Cook Time: 20min
Serving: 5

Ingredients

1. 1 lb. of pork tenderloin
2. 10 cups of mixed salad greens
3. 2 oranges, seedless, cut into bite-sized pieces
4. 1 tablespoon orange zest, grated
5. 2 tablespoons of cider vinegar
6. 2 tablespoons of olive oil
7. 2 teaspoons of Dijon mustard
8. ½ cup of an orange juice
9. 2 teaspoons of honey
10. ½ teaspoon of ground pepper

Directions

1. A bowl should be used to combine all of the ingredients for the dressing.
2. At a temperature of medium, grill the pork for nine minutes on each side while covering it.
3. After five minutes, then slice.
4. Tenderloin should be sliced very thinly.
5. Keep the greens on the plate that you will be serving them on.
6. Oranges and bacon should be placed on top.
7. Optional: sprinkle some nuts on top.

Nutritions

Calories 211
Carbohydrates 13 gram

Cholesterol 51 milligrams
Fiber 3 gram
Sugar 0.8 gram
Fat 9 gram
Protein 20 gram
Sodium 113 milligrams

Barley Veggie Salad

Prep Time: 10min
Cook Time: 20min
Serving: 6

Ingredients

1. 1 tomato, seeded and chopped
2. 2 tablespoons of parsley, minced
3. 1 yellow pepper, chopped
4. 1 tablespoon of basil, minced
5. ¼ cup of almonds, toasted
6. 1¼ cups of vegetable broth
7. 1 cup of barley
8. 1 tablespoon of lemon juice
9. 2 tablespoons of white wine vinegar
10. 3 tablespoons olive oil
11. ¼ teaspoon of pepper
12. ¼ teaspoon of salt
13. 1 cup of water

Directions

1. Put the water, barley, and broth into a pot and bring to a boil.
2. Remove the heat. After covering it, allow it to simmer for ten minutes.
3. Remove from the heat temporarily. In the meantime, transfer the tomato, parsley, and

yellow pepper to a bowl and mix them together.

4. Mix the barley into the mixture. Vinegar, oil, basil, lemon juice, water, pepper, and salt are all mixed together in a basin using a whisk.
5. To your barley mixture, pour this over it. Mix thoroughly by tossing.
6. Prior to serving, give the almonds a slight stir.

Nutritions

Calories 211
Carbohydrates 27 gram
Cholesterol 0 milligram
Fiber 7 gram
Sugar 0 gram
Fat 10 gram
Protein 6 gram
Sodium 334 milligram

Potato Calico Salad

Prep Time: 15min
Cook Time: 5min
Serving: 14

Ingredients

1. 4 red potatoes, peeled and cooked
2. 1½ cups of kernel corn, cooked
3. ½ cup of green pepper, diced
4. ½ cup of red onion, chopped
5. 1 cup of carrot, shredded
6. ½ cup of olive oil
7. ¼ cup of vinegar
8. 1½ teaspoons of chili powder
9. 1 teaspoon salt
10. Dash of hot pepper sauce

Directions

1. A jar should be used to store all of the ingredients together.
2. Close it and give it a good shake. Put the potatoes in cubes.
3. Include the carrot, onion, and corn in the salad bowl, and combine with the cabbage.

4. Spread the dressing over the top.
5. Now give it a light toss.

Nutritions

Calories 146
Carbohydrates 17 gram
Cholesterol 0 milligram
Fiber 0 gram
Sugar 0 gram
Fat 9 gram
Protein 2 gram
Sodium 212 milligram

Asian Crispy Chicken salad

Prep Time: 10min
Cook Time: 10min
Serving: 2

Ingredients

1. 2 chicken breasts halved, skinless
2. ½ cup of panko bread crumbs
3. 4 cups of spring mix salad greens
4. 4 teaspoons of sesame seeds
5. ½ cup of mushrooms, sliced
6. 1 teaspoon of sesame oil
7. 2 teaspoons of canola oil
8. 2 teaspoons hoisin sauce
9. ¼ cup of sesame ginger salad dressing

Directions

1. The chicken breasts should be flattened to a thickness of half an inch.
2. Mix the hoisin sauce and the sesame oil together. Coat the chicken with the sauce.
3. Crispy from Asia! A bowl should be used to combine the panko and the sesame seeds. Proceed to dip the chicken mixture into it.
4. Five minutes should be spent cooking each side of the chicken.
5. In the meantime, split the salad greens between two dishes and set them aside.
6. Add some mushrooms on top.
7. Cut the chicken into pieces and keep it on top. Add the dressing in a drizzle.

Nutritions

Calories 386
Carbohydrates 29 gram
Cholesterol 63 milligram
Fiber 6 gram
Sugar 1 gram
Fat 17 gram
Protein 30 gram
Sodium 620 milligram

SOUP AND STEW

Meatball stew

Prep Time: 15min
Cook Time: 25min
Serving: 2

Ingredients

1. 1 lb of sausage meat
2. 2 cups of chopped tomato
3. 1 cup chopped vegetables
4. 2 tablespoons of Italian seasonings
5. 1 tablespoons of vegetable oil

Recipe

1. Roll the sausage into meatballs.
2. Put the Instant Pot on Sauté and fry the meatballs in the oil until brown.
3. Mix all the ingredients in your Instant Pot.
4. Cook on Stew for 25 minutes.
5. Release the pressure naturally.

Nutritions

Calories 300
Carbs 4 gram
Sugar 1 gram
Fat 12 gram
Protein 40 gram
GL 2 gram

Sweet and sour soup

Prep Time: 15min
Cook Time: 35min
Serving: 5

Ingredients

1. 1 lb cubed of chicken breast
2. 1 lb chopped of vegetables
3. 1 cup low carb sweet and sour sauce
4. ⅕ cup diabetic marmalade

Recipe

1. Get all the ingredients together Mix all the ingredients in your Instant Pot.
2. Cook on Stew for 35 minutes.
3. Release the pressure naturally.

Chickpea Soup

Prep Time: 15min
Cook Time: 35min
Serving: 2

Ingredients

1. 1 lb of cooked chickpeas
2. 1 lb of chopped vegetables

3. 1 cup of low sodium vegetable broth
4. 2 tablespoons of mixed herbs

Recipes

1. Mix all the ingredients in your Instant Pot.
2. Cook on Stew for 35 minutes.
3. Release the pressure naturally.

Nutritions

Calories 310
Carbs 20 gram
Sugar 3 gram
Fat 5 gram
Protein 27 gram
GL 5 gram

French Onion Soup

Prep Time: 30min
Cook Time: 30min
Serving: 2

Ingredients

1. 6 onions, chopped finely
2. 2 cups of vegetable broth
3. 2 tablespoons of oil
4. 2 tablespoons of Gruyere

Recipe

1. Place the oil in your Instant Pot and cook the onions on Sauté until soft and brown.
2. Mix all the ingredients in your Instant Pot.
3. Cook on Stew for 35 minutes.
4. Release the pressure naturally.

Nutritions

Calories 110
Carbs 8 gram
Sugar 3 gram
Fat 10 gram
Protein 3 gram
GL 4 gram

Lemon-Tarragon Soup

Prep Time: 10min
Cook Time: 10min
Serving: 2

Ingredients

1. 1 tablespoon of avocado oil
2. ½ cup of diced onion
3. 3 garlic cloves, crushed
4. ¼ plus ⅛ of teaspoon sea salt
5. ¼ plus ⅛ of teaspoon
6. Freshly ground black pepper
7. 1 (13.5-ounce) can full-fat coconut milk
8. 1 tablespoon freshly squeezed lemon juice
9. ½ cup raw cashews
10. 1 celery stalk
11. 2 tablespoons chopped fresh tarragon

Directions

1. It is recommended to heat the avocado oil in a skillet of medium size over medium-high heat.
2. Saute the onion, garlic, salt, and pepper for three to five minutes, or until the onion is tender, depending on how long you sauté it.
3. The onion mixture should be blended with the coconut milk, lemon juice, cashews, celery, and tarragon in a high-speed blender until the mixture is completely smooth.
4. Should it be required, adjust the seasonings.
5. You can either move the mixture to a medium saucepan and cook it over low heat for three to five minutes before serving it, or

you can fill one large or two small dishes and enjoy it right away.

Nutritions

Calories 60
Carbohydrates 13 gram
Protein 0.8 gram

Chicken Zoodle Soup

Prep Time: 15min
Cook Time: 30mi
Serving: 2

Ingredients

1. 1 lb of chopped cooked chicken
2. 1 lb of spiralized zucchini
3. 1 cup of low sodium chicken soup
4. 1 cup of diced vegetables

Recipe

1. Mix all the ingredients except the zucchini in your Instant Pot.
2. Cook on Stew for 35 minutes.
3. Release the pressure naturally.
4. Stir in the zucchini and allow to heat thoroughly.

Nutritions

Calories 250
Carbs 5 gram
Sugar 0 gram
Fat 10 gram
Protein 40 gram
GL 1 gram

CONCLUSION

You've been taken on a culinary adventure by "FAST AND SIMPLE DIABETES RECIPES COOKBOOK: Delicious and Healthful Recipes for Managing Diabetes," which aims to make diabetes management more pleasurable, easy, and savory. We've looked at a wide range of recipes in this cookbook that not only satisfy the nutritional requirements of people with diabetes but also highlight the satisfaction that comes from eating healthfully. Every recipe, from filling breakfasts to satisfying lunches, from healthy snacks to delicious dinners, and even from decadent desserts, has been meticulously developed to guarantee that it satisfies the dietary requirements necessary to maintain stable blood sugar levels. The focus has been on utilizing high-quality, fresh ingredients and clever cooking methods that improve each dish's flavor and health advantages. Busting the misconception that a diet for people with diabetes must be bland or restricted has been one of the main objectives of this cookbook. We've shown you can have a rich and varied diet and still effectively manage your diabetes by exhibiting a wide variety of flavors, textures, and cuisines. These recipes are made to fit easily into your lifestyle, whether you have been treating diabetes for years or are just starting out. They are convenient without sacrificing flavor or quality. Apart from offering delectable recipes, our objective is to provide you with knowledge and self-assurance in your cooking decisions. Achieving and maintaining optimal health requires knowing how different foods affect your blood sugar levels, balancing carbohydrates with proteins and healthy fats, and reaping the benefits of varied cooking techniques. This cookbook's recipes are quick and easy to make since it recognizes that time is of the essence in today's hectic world. Our aim is to facilitate the adherence to a diabetes-friendly diet by providing simple and quick meal ideas, even on your busiest days. Every dish has been tried and tested for ease of preparation, so you can make delicious meals with the least amount of work and the most benefit. Recall that maintaining an overall healthy lifestyle is just as important for managing diabetes as what you eat as you proceed on your path to improved health. Your well-being is largely influenced by getting enough sleep, controlling stress, engaging in regular physical activity, and drinking plenty of water. To get the best results, we advise you to utilize this cookbook in conjunction with other healthful behaviors, as it is just one tool in your toolbox. With confidence and inventiveness, we hope that "FAST AND SIMPLE DIABETES RECIPES COOKBOOK" has motivated you to take charge of your health. You can enjoy a delicious and satisfying diet that helps you achieve your diabetes control objectives if you use the recipes and advice offered. Always keep in mind that every little step you take now toward eating well will pay off later on in life. We appreciate you coming along on this gastronomic journey with us. Cheers to many more scrumptious dinners and a long, happy, healthy life!

Printed in Great Britain
by Amazon